RAISING A HAPPY DOG:
THE ULTIMATE DOG TRAINING GUIDE FOR A HAPPY AND WELL-TRAINED DOG

ROBERT A. NOTO

TABLE OF CONTENTS

A dog is the only thing that can mend a crack in your broken heart - Judy Desmond

INTRODUCTION

Getting a new puppy into your life is one of the most thrilling things you can do in this world. And if it's a puppy, even better! Puppy dogs are the sweetest things ever. There isn't a single person alive, in my opinion, who doesn't melt when they hold a puppy in their arms.

They are often small mischief makers, however. They need to learn limits just as kids do. They are unable to resist acting like puppies. You must instruct them on how to behave like a dog. But it's worth it for your dog. Dogs are extremely kind in return! The path entails much more than just having a friend in your life.

We can learn so much from dogs. They never harbor grudges, love unconditionally, live in the now, and are never vindictive.

Putting this aside, owning a dog does come with its share of difficulties.
To live in peace with your dog, you will need to teach your new companion several things.
Building a satisfying connection with your dog is made easier by training.
However, relax since you are in capable hands.

You should use this puppy training manual. You will get all the knowledge required to train your puppy to behave properly.

We're cutting to the chase with each chapter's extreme practicality.

Here are some of the topics we'll be discussing:

Understanding your puppy's body language; can help you get inside his thoughts. You'll also

learn about crate training and why you should teach your dog this skill. Finally, you'll learn how to teach your puppy the five most crucial commands: "Sit," "Stay," "Lie Down," "Recall," and "Heel."
Housebreaking, teaching your puppy manners, and teaching them to stop biting, leaping, and barking excessively, among many other topics are covered in this guide.

An attentive puppy is a joy to be around.
So, let's dive in.

Chapter 1

BEGINNING THE PROCESS OF PUPPY TRAINING

Getting your puppy to pay attention to you is the goal of puppy training. Knowing what to teach your dog, when to educate it, and how to teach it are crucial.

Training your dog begins as soon as you bring him home. Whatever your dog does, you must respond appropriately, otherwise, he may wind up picking up the incorrect habits. Although you may certainly be looking forward to the benefits of owning a puppy, it won't be easy. Puppies are adorable, curious little bundles of joy who are fun to be around. It may sometimes get frustrating, however. The housebreaking process will go more quickly and without stress, if you are prepared to handle the obstacles that come with having a new puppy in the house.

When parenting a puppy, there are a few things you should do right.

The puppy might feel more secure with routines. For instance, his food and water dishes should always be put in the same location.

You must establish a daily schedule for your puppy, including where his food dish should be, when he should eat, where his bed should be, what time he should get up, when he should use the restroom, and when he should go for walks or playtime.

It would be incorrect to assume that how these exercises are taught doesn't affect them. It is significant. Your puppy will be well-behaved and content if you use the proper education strategy. Your puppy will start making his own choices and attempt to fit you into his life if you adopt improper teaching techniques. The order should be reversed.

Teach Through Words

After your dog has mastered the two most crucial words, you should teach them a few other words. These are the two words:

"NO," and "GOOD,"

You must educate your dog on more than simply the routines. You'll also need to teach it words. Anytime your puppy does something you like, let them know by saying "good," and if they do something you don't like, tell them "no." When your dog is around two months old, you may start with this. Proper instruction should be given using these words. Your tone and body language have a huge impact. If your puppy is older than three months old when you receive it, you should start teaching them these two words right away.

Avoid training with treats

Dogs adore goodies. But it's best to refrain from rewarding excellent conduct with rewards. Treats alone should not be used to teach your dog. You may be curious.
What is incorrect with it? When you begin "biscuit training," you are transferring decision-making authority to your puppy. Your puppy will determine whether or not to listen to you. This gives your puppy the impression that he does not need to pay attention to you.

This does not imply that you should completely stop giving your dog treats.
Treats may help motivate animals, particularly when teaching them new behaviors. However, this ought to be a reward rather than the teaching strategy itself. A dog cannot be trained by constantly coaxing him to perform what you want.

Respect Training

Only if your puppy respects you will he pay attention to you. Your dog needs to understand that you are in charge at home. Your dog could pick up the phrases and routines if you treat him disrespectfully, but he won't pay attention to you. Ineffective training is to blame for your puppy's contempt. It will also occur if you are coddled too much. If you want your dog to pay attention to you, he has to learn who the head of the household is. You cannot achieve respect nearly perfectly.

Consistency is necessary, and you should continue doing it often.

This book will assist you in understanding the issues in this respect.

A dog may pick up a lot of words, so picking the ones you want him to learn intentionally is the best approach to help him comprehend what you want him to do and what you don't. If you don't know how to teach, knowing the words you wish to teach won't help. You shouldn't anticipate that your dog will pay attention to your child's story. He will, however, pay close attention to what you have to say. He should be enthusiastic to carry out your instructions.

Crate Training

When your puppy is two to three months old, you may begin teaching him to use a crate. When you wish to housebreak your puppy, a crate will assist keep your dog from having accidents in the house. Your dog's haven would be in the crate. Do not consider this to be a dog's prison. If you do, your dog will begin to think similarly.

Your dog may not like having his mobility limited at first. But it won't be long before he goes to his kennel by himself to take a sleep or simply to get away from the chaos of the home. A kennel for a new puppy

will serve as a sleeping area for him as well as a means of aiding with housebreaking. It becomes quite simple to transport your puppy to the veterinarian or even on road trips once he becomes used to the crate.

Housebreaking

You may start housebreaking training your dog at two to three months old. A two-month-old dog is comparable to a newborn child. Their bladder control won't be that strong. especially a puppy of a tiny breed. For many months, they struggle to gain bladder control. However, as soon as your puppy arrives at your house, you should begin housebreaking activities.

A pattern should be established first. This will also encourage your puppy to comply with you. Housebreaking will be nothing short of a nightmare if you do this incorrectly, however. The majority of owners do not become aware of it until their dog has had an accident inside. It will start to seem regular to have accidents, and it will be quite hard to break this behavior.

There are several approaches you might take to control this. For smaller breeds, this can include using a litter box, a doggie door, or even a cage.

Acceptance

You must begin handling your puppy as well. He would only agree to anything you did with him in this manner. You must establish yourself as the household's alpha dog for your puppy. Being the leader doesn't mean you have to constantly make judgments about what is and isn't appropriate for your dog. For instance, bathing your dog, cleaning its teeth, trimming its nails, putting on a collar or leash, or even giving it medicine. You get to decide on what has to be done in these situations, not your dog. The ideal method to do this would be to include some respect-related teachings with the vocabulary instruction. If you teach the puppy the words and you are respected in return, acceptance will come.

Gentleness

Additionally, you must educate your puppy that being around people requires him to be nice. He must refrain from nibbling or chewing on people's hands or feet. Similar to acceptance training, your dog has to learn how to be kind. When a mother firmly corrects her puppy while the dog is playing, she typically teaches the puppy to be kind. Your task is to take control at that point. You are the parent of your puppy.

Therefore, it's not enough to just care for the puppy; you also need to discipline him when he begins acting inappropriately. You must educate your dog to exercise restraint.
You get to decide what is acceptable and unacceptable conduct. Remember this.

House Rules

You'll need to educate your puppy on the appropriate and inappropriate habits for the home. Can he gnaw on the shoes? No. Is he permitted to sit on the furniture or jump on people's laps while others are around? This is up to you to decide, and everyone in the home should abide by your decision.

same also Is it okay for him to go inside the kitchen while the meal is cooking? No, presumably because this may be dangerous for your Puppy. Simple things like whether or not he is permitted to pull socks out of the laundry pile, spend the night in your bed, or even bark at visitors from the window.
You must establish the rules for the home and then enforce them consistently so that your puppy learns to obey you.

Inform the other residents of the residence as well if you consider anything unacceptable. Your pet shouldn't be perplexed.

Advice for Older Dogs

You may assume that an older puppy will have a different training program.
It's not. The puppy should get the same training regimen regardless of age. Starting with vocabulary practice is necessary. Begin with the fundamentals, including routine, reward, reprimands, crate training, acceptance training, kindness, and even home rules. Therefore, this would be a good time to start the fundamental training if your puppy is still eating from your hand, barking at strangers, or resisting your commands to stop. Before going on to terms like remain, sit, or even heel, start with the basic and important phrases No and Good. Regardless of his age, respect must always come first.

When he has mastered the fundamental terms, go on to others. Such as not pulling on the leash while walking, coming to you when called, laying down or being still, waiting at the door even while it is open, ceasing his barking when instructed to do so, and many other things. Your dog would have to learn new terms to do all these tasks. It is important to put these terms into practice as well as grasp their meanings.

These words must be taught in a certain way. Your puppy will see you as a leader if you do this. Treating him won't do him any good.

Note, that being a leader does not include striking your dog or wearing a choker. You will need to say and perform a few little things while dealing with your dog. Every puppy will act inappropriately sometimes.
The way you react to them, however, really does make a difference.

If you keep giving the incorrect response, the dog will keep acting out. He will see you as the leader if you answer favorably. If you can get this right from the start, all the better. You have the opportunity to educate a new puppy on all the good behaviors and to discipline him when he behaves improperly.

Chapter 2

WHAT A PUPPY THINKS ABOUT

Have you ever wondered what your dog is thinking?

Do you want to know what your dog may be thinking? Isn't that something to be desired? You may have imagined a scenario in which your dog could effectively communicate with you. Unfortunately, this is only wishful thinking. You may, however, get a fundamental knowledge of your puppy's mind.

Staring

Your pet is staring at you wistfully, and you may be wondering, "What are you thinking?" It could be quite tough to understand what he is thinking if you have previously fed him and taken him for a walk. Dogs often direct their intense stare onto their owners. This probably doesn't indicate boredom. He probably has his eyes glued to you because he needs a reward, wants to play, or simply needs some long-lasting pet time. Your dog may be acting off because he needs more love and care.

Downcast

Do you feel awful leaving your dog home alone while you spend the whole day at work? You may be concerned that your dog will be depressed all day. Your puppy will be OK unless it suffers from separation anxiety.
The puppy would welcome the dog walker with a wagging tail if you had a dog walker checking on your dog. When you leave, your puppy could seem bewildered or even unhappy, but they usually become acclimated to your routine. They often adjust to it. But your dog must recognize the difference between your regular work routine and a lengthy getaway.

Barking Frequently

Does your dog typically howl all night long? It can seem that the main goal of his actions is to prevent you from sleeping. You must keep in mind that they bark for a specific cause. Your dog isn't barking at you to irritate you. This may be your puppy's attempt to grab your attention.

A dog often barks to communicate its desires. Maybe a treat, the chance to take a stroll, or even the chance to be let free. Another explanation is that your dog is trying to warn you because he perceives danger. Either that, or he's giddy and wants to play with you. Dogs often imitate their habits to learn. If your puppy learns that he can obtain what he wants by barking, he will continue to do so.

Head bobbing

When you talk to your dog, you may have observed that he often tilts his head to the side. There is no way that your dog understands the narrative you are providing him as the reason for this. For a variety of reasons, they often cock their heads. Your dog may be trying to comprehend a word you are saying or a familiar sound better.

Additionally, your puppy may be cocking his head to improve his hearing. maybe to get a better view of your face so they can make out what you are saying.

It's a lifelong endeavor to try to comprehend what goes on in your puppy's head. After some practice, you'll be able to tell what your dog wants by the expression on its face.

Chapter 3

BENEFITS OF CRATE TRAINING

Using a container has a lot of advantages. It is useful whether you are bringing your dog to the veterinarian, a kennel, a hotel, or even while you are flying.
It's beneficial to teach your dog to utilize a crate. Let's examine the advantages that using a crate might bring you and your dog.

Facilitates Housebreaking

Puppies naturally feel denting since it is a quality they received from their ancestors. This implies that they would maintain their den, where they live and eat, free of feces and urine. This may be used to shorten the housebreaking process for your dog and prevent any minor mishaps.

Your dog will undoubtedly delay using the restroom as long as they can after you have put them in the crate. Your dog may spend a little time in the crate before being sent outside to use the restroom.

Encourage them, and they'll execute the action for sure. As a result, they would wait for you to take them outdoors rather than wandering the house and defecating wherever they pleased.

Agonizing Chewing Is Slowed

The majority of dogs, both pups and adults, chew often, particularly while they are teething. It's crucial to educate them on what they should and shouldn't chew if you want to keep your home stuff intact. Your dog will develop a habit of chewing on things if it is let to do it frequently. If your dog habitually chews on shoes, slippers, pillows, or anything else, it will become a habit for him.

You may instruct your puppy to chew on something more appropriate if you are watching your dog and see this activity. But if you can't supervise them, you may put them in the crate with their chew toys. By doing this, you may train your dog to chew just on appropriate toys and stop them from gnawing on inappropriate ones.

It protects your dog

Keep your puppy in their box if you can't watch them all the time because there are many possibilities for them to get into mischief of any kind. Getting into trouble might entail damaging your possessions or putting yourself in danger.

Stops the Development of Problem Behaviors

Dogs enjoy looking for rewards. They will act in a variety of ways until they discover the one that will assist them in their pursuit of a prize. To continue receiving the incentive, the puppy will repeat the same behavior in the future. They develop their behaviors in this way. For you, it would be unpleasant for the dog to dig in the yard or devour everything in the refrigerator. You may alter their conduct if you have a chance to catch them.

But what should it do while you're not around? To prevent your dog from engaging in any undesirable behaviors when you aren't around, crate training is recommended. The amount of time they spend in the box will gradually become shorter as they get older.

Security and Safety

Your dog would have a particular space in a crate. They would have their own space in a cage, where they could unwind and sleep in peace.
Its den is the container. A dog would feel in its box the same way a kid would in their room.

To address behavioral issues

The behavioral issues with your dog may be resolved through training and control.
Your dog has to be trained to cease any bad behavior and be taught proper conduct. The goal of management is to eliminate any opportunities for your pup to engage in undesirable behavior. This combination will aid in discouraging any bad conduct in your dog

and reinforcing good behavior. When you can't stop your puppy from acting in a bad way, you may put them in a crate.

Keep your Puppy calm

A box would be the ideal object for a time-out. The crate is the greatest choice if you need to remove your puppy from a situation to calm them down from their overexcited condition. When playing with another dog or even while engaging in any vigorous game with you, they may become overly excited.

Travel safely

Your dog will need to be created for flight travel. They will be more at ease and prepared for the adventure if they are used to being in crates. While in a vehicle, they don't necessarily need to be created, although it will be best if they are. In the event of an automobile collision, an unrestrained dog may sustain harm. Additionally, he could crawl out the window and distract the driver.

travel without incident and safely. It aids in housebreaking and gives the puppy his area to escape. Crate Training doesn't take very long.

Chapter 4:

CRATE TRAINING

The several advantages of crate training were covered in the previous chapter.
Let's start with the fundamentals of crate training in this chapter.

Introduce The Crate

Your puppy most likely hasn't spent much time in a crate before, except when he had to travel or when the breeder began housebreaking him. As a result, your dog will be unaccustomed to crate training. The only factor that makes it work is your puppy's natural desire to keep his den tidy. The pups would leave their den in the wild to relieve themselves. Even if it meant just moving into the wilderness in two steps. Their minds are programmed with this instinct. Most likely, your dog has never seen a true den. They will act instinctively while in a crate, therefore he will make every effort to keep it clean.

Housebreaking a dog is undoubtedly much simpler with crate training. A puppy will always like to remain close to his group. You are now his pack, I guess. If he were far from you, he would be worried. This might be the cause of your puppy's crying, whining, or even commotion while he is in his crate. He doesn't mind the box; he simply feels exposed without you. Although it doesn't yet realize it, your dog is secure there. Because he is a domestic dog, it will take some time for your puppy to become accustomed to being alone.

Before allowing your dog to spend time inside the crate, you should just let him get used to it. Never use the crate as a means of punishment when crate training your dog. His haven must be the container. It must serve as his haven. If you use it as a kind of discipline, he won't think highly of it. It must be where your dog feels most at ease. Here are some guidelines and suggestions to help your dog adjust to his new kennel.

Open access is necessary. You should first leave the crate's door open.

Open the crate and add some snacks inside. A puppy will explore the kennel and devour his rewards out of curiosity.

Additionally, you may feed your puppy within the kennel. In doing so, the puppy will be assisted in creating a connection between meals and his crate. Although it could seem a bit uncomfortable at first, the puppy will become used to feeding within the crate. Playing a game of hiding and seek with your dog might help make crate training seem enjoyable. Ask your dog to discover a toy or reward that you've hidden within the kennel. "Where's your treat?" is an encouraging phrase you may use. Let's search for it! You'll need to encourage him to discover it after doing so. You may say something like, "Oh look! your package is inside! Oh, good boy!

Safety in Crate Training

Your dog will be safer inside of a crate. Here are a few ways you may ensure that he remains secure there, however. Never tie your dog to a chain when putting him in the kennel.

Also, keep away from slip collars. These items often get entangled in situations. He'll get anxious as a result, and things can turn out very badly. Make sure the collar is plain and unadorned.

Make sure the room or location where the puppy is kept has enough airflow while he is in the crate. Never put the puppy in direct sunlight, leave it in a hot room, or leave it in the vehicle on a hot day.

Make sure that kids don't torment your dog while you are crate training him.
Do not allow them to torment your puppy or poke their fingers through the wire of the crate. Your dog will feel intimidated by this, which might cause him to lash out without his own doing.

Chapter 5

HOW TO TEACH YOUR PUPPY ROUTINES

An established schedule aids in familiarizing your dog. Puppies are undoubtedly happy little animals. However, having a schedule in place for your puppy to feel safe throughout training is extremely helpful.

In addition to teaching your dog the rules, establishing a schedule will help. Additionally, it will aid in his understanding of what you want and do not desire. Keep in mind that bringing a puppy home involves a significant transition for the animal as well. You are removing the dog from his normal surroundings and putting him in a foreign location for him. Even the most self-assured puppies would flinch. A schedule helps in giving the puppy some kind of familiarity. Additionally, it aids in limiting surprises and hence lessens any stress the dog may have.

House Rules

Before bringing a puppy home, be sure that everyone in the family is on board with the established guidelines. Only if there is a lack of consistency will the puppy get confused. The dog will only get confused if one person allows him to jump onto the couch while the other gets upset with him for doing the same. Puppies need constancy to learn. Constantly changing the rules will only confuse your dog and hinder his capacity to learn. Decide in advance on the puppy's access to the furnishings and his sleeping area. You get to choose the fundamental guidelines, whether or not he would have a container. As soon as you've settled on these guidelines, make sure that everyone in the home is on board with them.

Bathroom Routine

A schedule will make it simpler for the puppy to understand what is expected of him. For toilet training, you should choose a spot that can be simply cleaned as well as conveniently accessed. Make sure everyone in the home is aware of the puppy's "go" location. Animals can get puzzled if you move their bathroom. If you keep it in one spot, the scent and the surroundings will teach the puppy what to anticipate.

You must plan appropriate potty breaks for your dog. The best times to do it are first thing in the morning, after lunch, in the afternoon, and just before bed at night. As your dog gets older, fewer breaks will be required of him. The puppy will learn to manage his bladder as he gets older. However, if you want to prevent any "accidents" in the home, make sure you are following a timetable at first. As often as you can, take him for walks, particularly after each meal while he is still learning.

Mealtime Routine

You must choose a time and place for your puppy's meals as well as a routine for them. Whether or not the puppy is permitted to take any snacks from the table should be decided. Regarding these issues, the whole family should agree.
You wouldn't want to make a decision just to find out later that kids have been feeding the

puppy undercover. Giving your dog any goodies from the table would be detrimental to both the puppy's health and training. Additionally, it would result in snatching food from the table and begging!
Ensure that nobody is feeding the puppy to tease it. This is something kids often do but shouldn't. You wouldn't be doing the dog any favors by insisting that he just consumes food from his dish while others sneak food to him. You may be able to reach a compromise. If family members decide to offer the puppy any leftovers, they should put them in his dish after he has finished his usual meal. These may be used for his training sessions as well.

Exercise Program

Plan your puppy's playtimes based on his energy level and playing style. Exercise is important for your puppy's health as well as for wearing him out. Playing with puppies aids in their connection with you. Use this playtime to introduce some fundamental obedience instructions. Every day, spend five minutes reviewing the lessons the puppy has previously learned. He may learn some new ones from you as well.

CHAPTER 6

THE 5 COMMANDS YOU MUST TEACH YOUR PUPPY

You may train your puppy to comprehend what you want him to do or not do by using commands. You may use commands to talk to your dog. Let's look at five fundamental instructions that you should teach your puppy in this chapter. Your dog should obey these orders to sit, stay, lie down, recall, and heel.

They will assist you in telling your dog what you want. Once you've finished teaching him these fundamental instructions, you may go on to more complex ones.

Teaching your puppy to sit

Initially, you'll need to train your puppy to sit when instructed to do so. Your dog is being courteous by sitting. This natural response demonstrates the dog's lack of aggression. It also demonstrates the puppy's capacity for patience.

When you reinforce this instruction, the puppy will learn that it is OK to sit and wait if he needs anything or if you are occupied. Teaching your dog this command can help him understand when to sit and pay attention or to just calm down.

You'll have to approach your dog directly. Be calm but firm. You must look your puppy in the eye and command him to sit before he will pay attention.
You may first hold a goodie slightly over your puppy's nose. Your dog will need to keep its head up to view the reward, and while he does so, his bum will drop.

As soon as your dog sits, praise him. You may respond "Yes" or "Good Boy" before giving him the promised reward. The idea is for your puppy to connect the action or phrase with the reward and the positive reinforcement it would provide.

Use hand gestures as often as possible rather than rewarding them with goodies. Once your dog is used to the spoken order, you may also communicate the same idea using a hand gesture. The most popular method is to say "Sit" while laying the flat of your palm over your dog's head and in front of it. Until your dog learns how to do it, you will need to keep doing this again. You'll need to be persistent and patient. Your dog must follow your example rather than vice versa.

'Stay' Command Training

One of the orders that can assist save your dog's life is "Stay," which is also one of the other commands that can achieve this. This order will aid in keeping your dog out of trouble and out of any potentially hazardous circumstances. Since staying is instinctual for puppies, they will have no trouble understanding the instruction. Your dog has to be taught how to "sit" before you can go on. You must stand facing the same direction as your dog when it sits. The "place" posture or position will be used to refer to this. The next step is to grip your dog's collar while saying its name and the word "Stay." Put your hand in front of the dog's face to do this. But it shouldn't go close to your dog. Your palm should be towards your dog, and your fingers should be pointing upward. Give your dog a treat and some praise if it remains motionless. If your dog gets up, repeat the process once again. Repeat the command until your dog learns what to do.

When your dog has mastered this command, you may move on to lengthening the duration that your dog spends doing so. Increase the amount of time your dog must remain motionless gradually. You will have to start again if your dog tends to stand up in the middle of the process. While your dog is motionless, you will also need to keep moving about. There should be a release word you may use to signal to your dog that it is now free to move. Words like "okay" or "come" are acceptable.

Teaching your puppy to lay down

Your dog has to be trained to lay down. The "Down" command should be used to halt whatever activity was being taken and is often used in conjunction with the "Stay" command.

occurring before the command was issued. The dog's conduct may be controlled or restrained with its aid.

The "Sit" command must be used first, followed by the name of your dog, then the command "Down." The palm of your left hand should be towards the floor when you hold it over your dog's head. Your right hand should be holding a goodie. Keep the hand close to your dog's body as you carefully lower it to the ground. You'll need to keep rewarding your dog in some way whenever he obeys this order.

You may praise your dog after it has positioned itself on the floor with its elbows and bum resting there. This will facilitate the development of a favorable link between the action taken and the benefit received. Until your dog truly masters this command, you will need to keep repeating it.

The objective is for your dog or puppy to pick up on the order and obey it. Regardless of what the command is, the dog must obey it. This will

enable you to intervene before your dog engages in any damaging behavior.
If your dog doesn't obey you, you'll have to start again, just like with any other command.

Teaching your puppy to recall

Your dog has to be trained to come to you at the sound of your voice. "Come" is another recalled word. You must first assume the fundamental "sit" stance before progressing. Start by calling your dog's name, then saying "Come," while gently tugging the dog by the collar. This should be said in an upbeat manner. To signal to your dog what you want it to do—come to you—you should accompany your command with a hand gesture. With the use of a reward or simply by laying some dog food at your feet and pointing at it, you may entice your dog to approach you.

Your dog will undoubtedly approach the food once you have gesticulated for a bit. It is crucial that you consistently provide your dog positive reinforcement so that he understands that what he is doing is the proper thing. The dog will

undoubtedly learn that what he is doing is desirable with the assistance of positive reinforcement and rewards. You will need to repeatedly practice this command.
Practice this command whenever you are engaging with your pet and whenever you get the chance. You'll have to start again if your dog decides to do anything else rather than approach you.

Teaching a Dog to Heel

One of the trickiest commands to teach your dog is probably this one. Your dog will eventually pick it up, however, given patience and persistence. The neck of your dog and your back, shoulders, and neck will all benefit from teaching your puppy to heel. Additionally, it will assist in preserving both your and your dog's dignity. Your dog, meanwhile, may not care all that much about decency. Your dog will likely want to move quickly, smell, and branch off in several directions. You'll have to let him know whether or not
He has to go spelunking now.

Put your dog in a sitting posture, to begin with. Get your dog to "sit" next to your leg by using the regular leash that you use to walk him. You should both be facing the same way. Utilize the left side to prevent confusing your dog. Say the name of your dog, then the word "heel." Say this as you take a forward stride with your left foot.

This will signal to your dog that it is okay to proceed. Your dog will either make an effort to stop or go quickly. If this happens, give his leash a little pull and give this order once again. You'll need to remind your dog to remain by your side repeatedly.

Say "Keep with me or over here" while patting your leg. Make sure to say "yes" when you do this. Your dog should be eager to obey your instructions.

In a very calm and authoritative voice, state your dog's name and command him to heel if he begins to walk in front of you. Pull on his leash if required, then request that he take a seat. If your dog struggles or advances, gently drag him over to where your left leg is. You and your dog shouldn't be tense with one another.

Your dog ought to be eager to obey you. Maintain your composure and be patient. It does take some time to perfect this command. Don't forget to compliment your dog every time he succeeds.

Additionally, you must train your dog to sit whenever you stop. When you feel like stopping, halt on your left foot and firmly command "sit." Your dog will undoubtedly get the hang of it after you repeat this many times. Practice giving this order using just your body language. Your dog will eventually comprehend what you mean. Depending on what works best, you may utilize spoken orders or physical gestures.

While training your dog, there are a few things you should keep in mind.
Never express any displeasure or annoyance you may experience during exercising. Your dog will just get confused or perhaps scared by this. Your dog will have a bad experience because of this, as well as you. Take a pause and restart if you sense that your composure is slipping away. Stay positive. Your dog should

experience rewards as well. Your dog needs you to be both tough and kind. Don't allow him to exploit you. The training sessions shouldn't be postponed, and you shouldn't give up too soon. The decision is yours, although teaching a puppy is simpler than training an adult dog.

Before you begin the training sessions, make sure the dog is aware of who is in charge. If the dog doesn't believe you are the leader, it won't listen to you. Finally, when it comes to teaching your dog, avoid involving too many people. The dog will get confused if it hears many things at once.

CHAPTER 7

HOUSEBREAKING YOUR PUPPY

Establishing a joyful and conflict-free connection with your dog starts with housebreaking them. You shouldn't allow the puppy out on its own until it has learned to use the bathroom. Your puppy must be housebroken with plenty of positive reinforcement, consistency, and patience. This practice aims to help your puppy develop some positive behaviors and establish a love connection with it. Your dog will likely need four to six months to become housebroken.

However, it could also take up to a year for certain pups. Size may also have a significant role. Compared to a larger puppy, a smaller puppy has a smaller bladder and a faster metabolism. A smaller puppy would thus need more frequent walks. The pup's living circumstances should also be taken into account. Additionally, you may need to change any bad behaviors your dog has and replace them with good ones. You'll need to make and follow a schedule.

Be patient

Additionally, you will need to be persistent and patient. Keep in mind that you are dealing with a puppy, who is illiterate in human language. A puppy just catches up on your nonverbal signals and tone of voice. You will undoubtedly experience some setbacks when teaching your puppy. You shouldn't give up on teaching the dog because of these difficulties. Your puppy will be OK as long as you continue to manage them. As soon as you see any indications that your puppy may need to urinate, you should take him outside, and you should praise him when he does potty outdoors. He will learn from this.

Beginning of Housetraining

Between the ages of 12 and 16 weeks, the puppy may begin housetraining. The puppy can manage his bowel and bladder functions at this age. You'll need more time to housebreak your puppy if you wait much longer. It may take longer for you to stop this practice and replace it with a positive habit if your puppy is used to urinating in his cage. Your puppy's house training will benefit from encouragement and rewards.

It's thought that limiting your puppy's access to space aids with housetraining. The puppy won't urinate in the same place where it eats or sleeps. He would thus want to go outdoors to relieve himself.

Here are some actions you can do to housebreak your puppy.

Establish a schedule.

For your puppy, you must create a routine and feed it according to that plan. In between meals, don't leave any food in the dog's dish. As soon as the puppy wakes up in the morning, after eating, when he awakens from sleep, and even after playing, take him for a walk. Every hour or so, take him outside to use the restroom.

Additionally, be careful to remove him from the house before he goes to sleep. Bring your dog to the same location each time so he may relieve himself. He will also be motivated to do so by the stench. Until he is taught to use the bathroom outdoors, you must remain with him. Every time your dog goes potty, you should compliment him or maybe offer him a reward. A stroll might also be enjoyable.

Employing a Crate

A crate is an additional option. Don't confine your puppy to the kennel for more than two hours at a time, however. Only let him spend the night time in the crate. The size of the container should be appropriate. If it's too huge, the dog could use it as a lavatory. He wouldn't feel comfortable if it were too little. If you are unable to stay with your puppy during the training process, you will need to find someone to watch after him and take him for walks while you are away from home. If you see that your puppy is going to the bathroom in the crate, you should cease using it.

The typical indications that your dog needs to go outside include sniffing the ground, barking, whimpering, circling, or scratching the door. During the potty-training process, accidents are inevitable. You must professionally handle these occurrences.

Don't yell at or be rude to your dog. Instead, properly clean the area and take the dog outdoors. Saying no as soon as you see the puppy getting ready to urinate can assist if you can keep an eye on it.

Chapter 8

HOW TO CORRECT BAD BEHAVIOUR

Any inappropriate conduct that the puppy exhibits must be corrected. Puppies are enthusiastic and bursting with energy. It is crucial to instill in them the concepts of right and wrong.

The lovely, cuddly puppy you brought home turns out to be a tiny monster that is trying to cause as much havoc as she can. You'll need to teach your puppy what it can and cannot do. It will be helpful if you have previously taught your dog some fundamental commands like sit, stay, come, and down before you begin addressing the undesirable behavior.

Rules for Dogs

Your dog needs constancy in his or her life. There must also be certain ground rules. The same approach should be used by every member of the household to teach or correct the puppy. If not taught, a dog—regardless of age—will behave in any way it pleases. Every time you reprimand your dog's conduct, you must maintain your composure. You shouldn't beat the dog or yell, scream, or shout at it. Your dog shouldn't be afraid of you.

Educating Your Dog

Any kind of negative behavior may be corrected with basic obedience training. Your pet has to be taught so that he is aware of the fundamental hand- or voice instructions.
When your puppy is three to four months old, you should do this. All the instructions that you have read about in the prior chapters should be covered in basic training. You may teach your puppy to sit when it is around 10 weeks old. A puppy as early as 10 weeks old may be trained with the aid of obedience experts. Additionally, these sessions will aid in your puppy's socialization with other dogs.
Biting and chewing, leaping up on humans, rough play, begging, excessive barking, and digging are all common dog behavior issues.

Let's examine each of them individually.
Avoid Having Your Dog Bite and Chew

The puppy's usage of his mouth during play is quite natural. He most likely did this with his littermates, and dogs will also do this to signal to other dogs or people to stop bothering them. Puppies often have very pointed teeth. It is important to avoid letting your Puppy bite you or mouthing your puppy at all times while you are playing with him.

You may do this by squealing a bit and uttering something like "ouch." The puppy will get alarmed and stop what he's doing as a result. Give him a treat or a toy instead of it anytime he stops, and praise him. If the dog does have teeth in your palm, simply scream and resist the urge to run away. He will stop biting once he sees this. When he does, immediately congratulate him. This will convey to him your satisfaction that he released your hand.

Any improper chewing your dog demonstrates must be stopped.

Puppies like to chew, particularly while they are teething. Furniture and shoes made of leather

are easy targets. Purchase quality chew toys and palatable chewables.
Your dog will learn what objects he can and cannot chew on thanks to this. He will gradually learn this and comprehend what is required of him.

Quit jumping!

A dog will often leap up on you when they are enthusiastic. When you return home, when guests arrive, or even when out for a stroll in the park, your dog could get excited. You can stop your dog from doing this in several different ways. By using the "Off" command, you may fix this in the best possible way. Your dog may be taught to do this in a very simple method.
Ask a member of your family or a friend to enter the room via the door.
Your dog has to be leashed and wearing a collar. Make your dog approach the door when the doorbell rings while keeping a tight grip on the leash to prevent the dog from leaping on the person answering the door. If he attempts to leap, you should pull on his leash, command

him to "off," and then command him to "sit." When he is sitting still and not attempting a leap, you may compliment him for being a nice boy. The alternative would be to just avoid eye contact with your dog. Continue doing this until your dog calms down, at which point you should give him praise.

Stopping Him From Playing Rough

When your dog begins to play rough, things may easily spiral out of hand and get hazardous. Never encourage your dog to bite you or any of your body parts. When your dog is a puppy, this could be cute, but it might harm someone else.
You should educate your dog to "drop it" whenever you play a game that requires force, like tug of war, so that he will cease what he is doing. You can stop pulling by saying, "Drop it." This ought to help. If not, you may issue the instruction, get up, and walk away. He will understand that if you play tough, you won't play with him.

Stop him from Begging

Most likely, your dog is always at your side. especially while you are in the middle of a meal. Most likely, the dog would do nothing except sit and look at you, pleading for food.
The most frequent explanation for this is that you may have unintentionally promoted this habit in the past. He feels it is OK for him to beg, thus you probably would have given him something that you were eating.

By feeding your dog at the same time as you eat and keeping him out of the space where you typically dine, you can eliminate this tendency. He may be kept outside the home or in his box. When he cries out, telling him flat-out no and telling him to sit and remain will help. It will take time to change this kind of behavior. So, when correcting him, be patient and persistent.

Excessive barking

You'll need to teach your dog the very crucial command "talk."

Offer him a reward to get him going, then instruct him to "talk". Every time he barks, reward him with a goodie. After he masters the talk command, teach him the word "silent." Get him to talk first before rewarding him this time. Instead, say "silent" while holding it in your hand. Reward him each time he stops barking. As a result, he will connect remaining silent with receiving a reward.

How to Manage Digging

Dogs have a natural tendency to dig. To avoid the heat and keep cool, many people like to excavate a space. There are many methods you may use to halt this behavior. He will get exhausted from vigorous exertion, and he won't dig. So that you can monitor him, you should keep him confined to the kennel in the yard or any other location that is fenced in. You may correct him as soon as he begins digging.

Wrap the hole with chicken wire (s). He will stop digging when he feels the texture of the chicken wire. His waste may also be used to plug the holes, which can then be covered with dirt. The scent of their excrement bothers dogs. So, that would be effective. You may instruct him on the regions in the yard where he is permitted to dig if you have any available space. Dogs sometimes tend to dig holes only to bury their bones. Don't let him chew his bones in the yard if that's the case.

Get Professional Assistance

Certain specialists can assist you with your dog if you ever need assistance correcting the behavior of your dog. Consult a veterinarian to rule out any potential medical causes for your dog's undesirable behavior.
You may contact dog trainers with the assistance of your veterinarian.

CHAPTER 9

ADVICE FOR TRAINING YOUR PUPPY

Your dog can begin training when he is old enough.
There is some advice that will aid you whether you are training the puppy on your own or with expert assistance. Be kind, understanding, consistent, and attentive to your puppy.
Let's look at some of the advice you should bear in mind when teaching your puppy in this chapter.

Take Your Puppy's Advice

You'll have to become used to paying attention to your dog. Don't force your puppy to say hello to people or other animals if they make him or her feel uneasy when meeting them. You must appreciate your dog's attempts to communicate with you that he feels uneasy. In the future, forcing this problem could lead to more serious problems.
Many affections

Most of the time, when humans get unhappy, they are incredibly adept at communicating their irritation to their dogs. They often overlook the nice things the dog does, however. This is a terrible error. Avoid doing this. When your dog behaves well, you should show your devotion, compliment him, and pay attention to him. He needs to be aware of his good character. At this point, you ought to be a bit more affectionate than usual.

Does your Dog Enjoy It?

It doesn't follow that your dog will immediately adore the snacks just because they are labeled "dog treats" on the packaging. Dogs choose their food carefully, much as people do. Therefore, keep an eye out and ascertain the kinds of items he adores.

Inform him of what to do

The "no" command may be used to instruct your dog not to do something. This doesn't provide your dog with a lot of information, however.

Tell him what you want him to do instead of simply saying "no."
Generalizations don't work well with dogs. Saying "no" wouldn't be much use if he jumps upon someone to meet them. He could go to the opposite side or leap a bit higher. Instead, instruct him on what to do after ceasing the activity he was doing. So advise him to sit down instead.
The puppy would get some understanding from it.

Be Consistent

Anytime you teach your dog, you must be consistent. When teaching your puppy, everyone in the household must be on the same page. Saying that something is unacceptable while allowing the dog to engage in the same behavior is inadmissible. The puppy will get perplexed.
Make sure you all speak to the dog using the same terms as well.
When asked to get up from the couch, someone might say "off" or "down." The dog

becomes extremely confused in such a situation. This should not be done.
attainable expectations

It takes a long time to alter behavior. You must have some reasonable expectations. The dog's undesired habits might take some time to be changed. The behaviors that dogs develop over time are often the ones that are hardest to break. Barking, digging, and greeting jumps are a few of these. Additionally, it depends on how much time the dog spends doing these skills.

You cannot expect to modify a habit in a short amount of time, for example, if your dog was trained to leap to welcome visitors and you let this continue for a long time. To change these behaviors and ingrain new ones requires time.

Healthy diet

The food you feed your dog has a significant impact. The diet needs to be based on how much exercise he gets.
For example, a dog used to herding sheep will require more protein than a dog that spends all

of its time indoors. Usually, a high-protein diet is beneficial. Ensure that your puppy becomes used to consuming dog food rather than human food. A healthy diet is crucial for your puppy's general welfare. Before starting any diet, see your veterinarian first.

Reinforcement

There is a very good chance that if your dog is engaging in actions that you don't like, they were previously rewarded.
For instance, you might toss the toy if your dog brought it to you and was barking at you to do so. Your dog is now aware that barking will result in his desires being met. Your dog begins to bark even more when you tell him to stop. If you cave, you could chuck it. Your dog will now think that perseverance is the key.
Therefore, you may instruct your dog to do something different rather than caving in. Most likely, you may ask him to sit or keep quiet.

Bribery Is Ineffective

Don't bribe your dog with goodies. Treats should be given as rewards, not as inducements to do certain actions. By doing this, you ultimately give the dog the ability to make decisions. At all costs, you should avoid doing this. Your dog will be allowed to make its own decisions about what it wants to do. Lessons should not be left up to the puppy's discretion; rather, they should be a learning exercise. When you desire, your dog should want to do the tasks you give it.

Freedom

Your dog should earn the right to be let inside. However, go gradually.
Most pet owners often allow their animals as much freedom as they wish. You are giving him too much independence too soon when you do this. Not only may this result in needless housebreaking mishaps, but it can also teach the puppy harmful behavioral habits. Use a baby gate to close off any vacant rooms if there are any.
Keeping your dog attached to you is the greatest method to ensure that he remains

secure. Start by demonstrating to him where he may feel secure and where you can keep an eye on him.

CHAPTER 10

CHOOSING THE RIGHT DOG

I can't conclude this book without mentioning the abundance of adult dogs searching for new homes in shelters around the country.
I like puppies just as much as everyone else, but I also have a special place for older dogs. My most recent two rescue pets were mature dogs.

Maybe it's because I believe they deserve another opportunity and I like being able to offer them a fresh start. After all, if you adopt an older dog, it was either rescued or was no longer able to be cared for by its previous owners.
Getting an older dog may be highly rewarding and entertaining! Also, it's positive karma.

Why Pick an Older Dog?

Let's start with the most crucial query before talking about breeds: why would you choose (and train) an adult dog over a puppy?

You firstly offer them an opportunity they would not have otherwise had. Dogs are pack animals and are sociable beings. Your family could be the perfect bundle for them!

Second, if you're new to the world of dogs or unsure of how your family and lifestyle will change, it's a smart idea to buy an older dog. While it's not always smooth sailing, older dogs are often less effortful than puppies, and you can tell right away about their size and temperament, so there are no unpleasant surprises.

Even a senior dog is an option. Senior dogs may be the most delightful companions, yet they are the most underappreciated breed in the world of rescue dogs.

With effort and patience, you can.
If you want a dog that is peaceful and has less energy, they are a fantastic option. Their reduced life expectancy and very high medical costs are the one thing you must be ready for.

Adult dogs are excellent friends in my opinion. I will have succeeded if my book motivates even one reader to adopt an elderly dog.

Be Upfront and Honest About What You Can Offer a Dog

Once you've decided to have a dog, the next thing to consider is what breed of dog would be the greatest for you.

It will be much simpler to choose the ideal breed if you are clear about the qualities you are looking for in a dog and what you can provide for it. Additionally, the fortunate dog that gets to accompany you home will be happy. Even though it may be tempting, selecting the puppy you think is the prettiest is just one part of choosing the ideal dog.

One of the "Dog Whisperer" reality TV shows, which aired on National Geographic, was fully devoted to so-called "wolfdogs." A domestic dog crossed with a wolf is known as a wolfdog. Since wolves have interested humans for countless years, some people find it intriguing

when they read an advertisement for a wolf puppy. They want to own a portion of nature. Wolfdogs also have a very adorable puppy face. But when pups become bigger, the owner soon realizes that this isn't your typical dog since wolves are predators and will go to great lengths to defend what they see as their owner's property. Instead of understanding that a wolfdog is merely acting by its nature, it often occurs that the owner believes his pet is acting inappropriately.
And before you know it, the wolfdog has been put to sleep in a cage or possibly taken to a shelter.

Although using wolfdogs as an extreme example, I hope you get the point: if you are clear about the kind of dog that would be a good fit for you, you are establishing the groundwork for a great marriage. And a lot of possible issues and annoyances will be avoided!
Therefore, if you lack energy, avoid getting a Jack Russell since they need a lot of walking.

Picking A Dog That's Right For You

Let's start with some questions and considerations you should think about:
A way of life. How do you prefer to live? Do you spend most of the day at home or do you work outside the home? You often travel, right? Where will your dog remain if you do that while you're not home? Do you lead a more active or sedentary lifestyle? Do you reside in a city or a rural area? These are all significant considerations when choosing the dog that is best for you.

Money: Dogs are pricey. They need food, immunizations, and expensive veterinary care if they get unwell. See your monthly spending to determine if you have enough money to pay for a dog comfortably.

A condominium or a home: You can use this to determine the size of dog you can keep. Additionally, you should confirm if dogs are permitted in your apartment complex.

Time off: How much free time can you offer your dog? Some breeds shouldn't be left alone since they need regular care.

It stimulates: Some breeds have a high level of intelligence and activity, characteristics that call for a lot of mental and physical activity. The breed that will work best for you depends on how much mental and physical exercise you can provide the dog.

Pedigree or mutt, etc: You may benefit from a pedigree by being aware of the temperament and defining traits of that specific breed. A mutt may be less predictable, but the danger of subsequently discovering unanticipated qualities is lower if you adopt or purchase one as an adult.

Cleaning up: You should think about the time you can dedicate to brushing your dog's coat. Some dogs, like the Hungarian Puli, have excessive amounts of hair or even dreadlocks, which need special care and consideration.

Additionally, certain breeds (like the Bulldog) are known for drooling and may leave smears of saliva all over the place. That's not meant to scare you away, simply to let you know how much cleaning and upkeep goes into caring for a dog.

You should give them a close examination so that you can choose what breed of dog is perfect for you. Even while owning a husky can be your dream, it's not the best option if you live alone in a tiny flat in the city and spend your days working outside the home.

You will be one step closer to welcoming your prospective canine companion into your house after you have a clear notion of the breed of dog that would be a suitable fit for you.

CONCLUSION

Bringing a puppy home is one of life's greatest joys. Those two intensely fixed eyes might make anybody smile. Even though they belonged to the dog who just wrecked the kitchen.

With the knowledge you've gained from this book, you now possess all the methods and tools necessary to teach your puppy and make him a well-behaved dog.

Here are some things you discovered:
How to teach your dog the five most crucial commands: The verbs "Sit," "Stay," "Lie Down," "Recall," and "Heel"
Understanding your dog's body language, housebreaking, crate training, and how to control undesirable behaviors like biting, leaping, and excessive barking are all covered in this book.

Training your dog will need some patience, time, and work. But I assure you, it's well worth it!

Start by practicing basic words. Teach your dog some simple vocabulary and instructions. Crate training may begin when this is finished.
Training in, acceptance, and respect needs to begin right away.
Start housebreaking as soon as you can since it takes time. You can start training your puppy some tricks after you have these things mastered. And always try to be patient with your puppy and don't give up.

Additionally, unknowingly, you are developing a bond with your puppy. It will learn what it can and cannot do if you set limits for him while treating him with love and care. It will also learn that you can be relied upon. He will repay you tenfold as well!

www.ingramcontent.com/pod-product-compliance
Lightning Source LLC
LaVergne TN
LVHW050337160826
845677LV00014B/3659

* 9 7 9 8 8 4 8 9 0 7 0 8 7 *